HAL•LEONARD
INSTRUMENTAL
PLAY-ALONG

AUDIO
ACCESS
INCLUDED

PLAYBACK+
Speed • Pitch • Balance • Loop

TRUMPET

THE BEATLES

T0081816

Cover Photo: Fiona Adams/Getty

To access audio visit:
www.halleonard.com/mylibrary

Enter Code
7089-8192-3937-2079

Audio Arrangements by Peter Deneff

ISBN 978-1-4950-9070-7

HAL•LEONARD®

7777 W. BLUEMOUND RD. P.O. BOX 13819 MILWAUKEE, WI 53213

In Australia Contact:
Hal Leonard Australia Pty. Ltd.
4 Lentara Court
Cheltenham, Victoria, 3192 Australia
Email: ausadmin@halleonard.com.au

Visit Hal Leonard Online at
www.halleonard.com

ALL YOU NEED IS LOVE

TRUMPET

Words and Music by JOHN LENNON
and PAUL McCARTNEY

BLACKBIRD

TRUMPET

Words and Music by JOHN LENNON
and PAUL McCARTNEY

DAY TRIPPER

TRUMPET

Words and Music by JOHN LENNON
and PAUL McCARTNEY

ELEANOR RIGBY

TRUMPET

Words and Music by JOHN LENNON
and PAUL McCARTNEY

GET BACK

TRUMPET

Words and Music by JOHN LENNON
and PAUL McCARTNEY

HERE, THERE AND EVERYWHERE

TRUMPET

Words and Music by JOHN LENNON
and PAUL McCARTNEY

HEY JUDE

TRUMPET

Words and Music by JOHN LENNON
and PAUL McCARTNEY

I WILL

Words and Music by JOHN LENNON
and PAUL McCARTNEY

TRUMPET

LET IT BE

TRUMPET

Words and Music by JOHN LENNON
and PAUL McCARTNEY

LUCY IN THE SKY WITH DIAMONDS

TRUMPET

Words and Music by JOHN LENNON
and PAUL McCARTNEY

OB-LA-DI, OB-LA-DA

TRUMPET

Words and Music by JOHN LENNON
and PAUL McCARTNEY

PENNY LANE

TRUMPET

Words and Music by JOHN LENNON
and PAUL McCARTNEY

SOMETHING

TRUMPET

Words and Music by
GEORGE HARRISON

TICKET TO RIDE

TRUMPET

Words and Music by JOHN LENNON
and PAUL McCARTNEY

YESTERDAY

TRUMPET

Words and Music by JOHN LENNON
and PAUL McCARTNEY